A LITTLE, BROWN BOOK

This book is dedicated to Roy who gave me the 'goal' and to Mary who made it 'home'.
Not forgetting Lynda who was almost overlooked in the rush for football.

Text and photographs © Stuart Clarke 1999

First edition

ISBN 0-316-64798-5

A CIP catalogue for this book is available from the British Library.

The author would like to thank the following people:

Our game's civil servants - The Football Trust; Football administrators - Gordon Taylor and The Professional Footballers Association, David Dent, Chris Hull and The Football League, Mike Foster and The FA Premier League (not forgetting Derek Johnstone), Alec McGivan and England 2006, Keith Cooper and F.I.F.A. ; Club Secretaries - John Alexander (Watford FC), Mark Blackbourne (Burnley FC, Sunderland FC); Clubs - Berkhamsted Dynamoes FC, Berkhamsted Eagles FC, Rotten End Harts FC, Coniston FC, Rift Valley Wanderers FC; Ground Builder Supreme - Paul Fletcher; A Pair of Players - Luther Blisset, Graeme Le Saux; Journalists - Graham Spiers, Ged Scott; Writer/Film-maker - Ian Fenton; Archivists - British Film Institute, Kodak; TV and Radio Presenters - Clare Tomlinson, Nick Barnes, Alan Green; Entertainers - Holding Back The Years Hucknall, Young Dudes Hunter, Yellow Brick Elton, Wildwood Weller, No Regrets Robbie, Crimson Trophies Willoughby; Teachers - Brian Bennett, Stewart Mann, Gus Wylie; Mentors - Big Uncle Al C and before him Per C; Assistants - Eleanor God Blimey; Helene and Andrew; Lile Ben; Business Colleagues - Mark Table Service Blackburn, Sue Hext, Richard Nelson; The Business Communities of Ambleside, Hawkshead, Grasmere and also Mauritius; In the City - Charles Manchester; In America - Douglas Messinger; Sponsors - Tim Bleakley, Talk Radio, EA Sports; Publishers - Julia Charles and Little, Brown and before them Howard Brown.

Designed by Wilson Design Associates

Little, Brown and Company
Brettenham House
Lancaster Place
London WC2E 7EN

Printed and bound in Italy

OPPOSITE: **THE BEGINNINGS OF A FOREST**
NOTTINGHAM FOREST 1993

The Homes of Football

the passion of a nation

Stuart Clarke

A CRACK AT BELLEVUE
DONCASTER ROVERS 1990

LEFT: **HALF MOON OVER WHITE HART LANE**
V NORWICH CITY, TOTTENHAM HOTSPUR 1990
The 'Spurs' field Gary plus Gazza, England's heroes from the World Cup summer ... the stuff of dreams.

**RIGHT: HORSE HATELEY'S ABUSIVE RETURN
V RANGERS, GLASGOW CELTIC 1997**
Made his name at Portsmouth... took his noble steed to
Scotland to become one of the greatest ever Rangers.
Then, heading towards retirement and on his way down the
ladder, a sudden recall for man Hateley who returns to taunt
the Celtic.

The match will erupt, with 'Hates' sent off.

**BELOW: TOMMY WAS CELEBRATES
BARNSLEY 1997**
Unfashionable, archetypal 4th-division Barnsley make it to
the Premier League!

Breasts are bared.

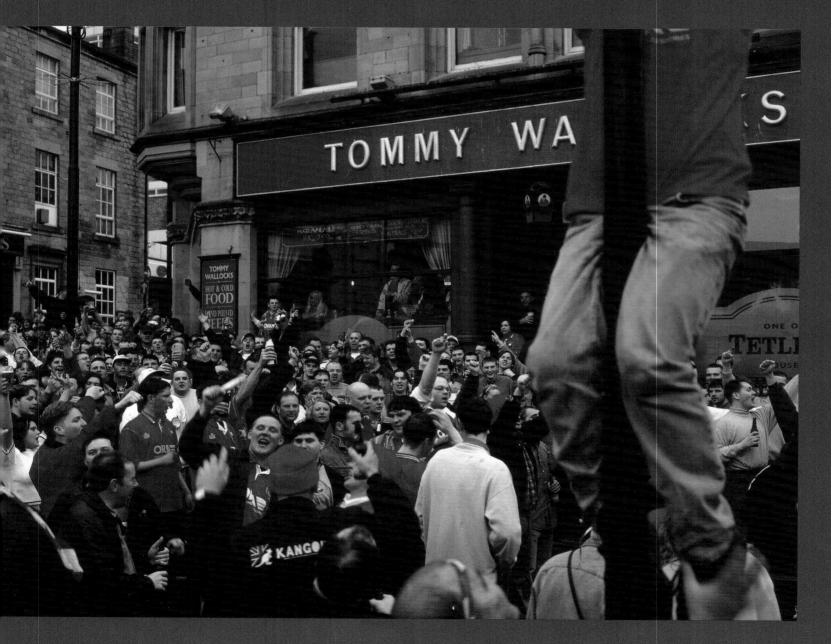

ABOVE: THE GATES OF CONVENIENCE
WORCESTER CITY 1991
Nowhere in England is far from the sea - and nowhere is
safe from its peculiar seaside (picture postcard) humour.

RIGHT: ALLEGIANCE TO THE WALL
GLASGOW RANGERS AT HAMPDEN PARK 1994
Even though, just a few yards away, toilets have been
installed at great cost at the National Stadium, the fans
do what comes naturally - handed down through
generations. Quite literally, it's in their genes.

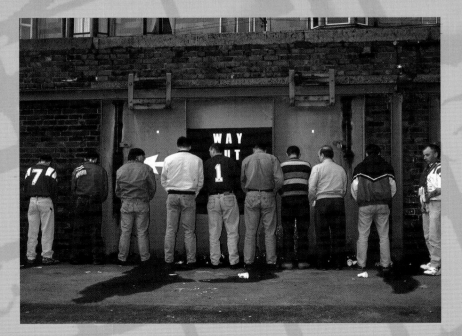

ABOVE: GOOD ABERDEENSHIRE STOCK
ABERDEEN V GLASGOW RANGERS (AT GLASGOW CELTIC) 1993
The Aberdeen-ies seem more than willing to go along with the
image the rest of the country has of them.

ABOVE: ALL THE WAY FROM ABERDEENSHIRE
ABERDEEN V GLASGOW RANGERS (AT GLASGOW CELTIC) 1993
The girl is told about their reputation...

ABOVE: CELTIC RIDE
GLASGOW CELTIC 1998
Their luck is in.

MAIN PICTURE: CELTIC SURGE
HEART OF MIDLOTHIAN 1997
Perhaps this will be Hearts season. Then the
auld firm move up an extra gear.

ABOVE: COMPLETELY DRUNK
GLASGOW CELTIC 1998
Finally a season of Championship triumph after 9 (nine) blue ones
without. An excuse for a bevvy.

ABOVE: THE SHAGGING (GRAND) STAND
DALBEATTIE STAR 1996
The morning after the night before - and the stand has (once again) been broken in to.

LEFT: GRAFFITTI IN THE SHAGGING STAND
DALBEATTIE STAR 1996
The usual suspects...

**RIGHT: MET THEIR MATCH ON LOVE STREET
ST. MIRREN 1996**
A footballing Saturday. The match is well underway.
Either the kids can't afford the admission ... or St.
Mirren are just so repulsive that they find better things
to pursue for 90 minutes.

**BELOW: PITCH TO PRACTICE ON
CRAIGMARK BURNTONIANS 1996**
Knees are scarred for life in this harsh arena. Ayrshire
is synonymous with men, mines and its footba'.

ABOVE: SOMEWHERE IN DERBYSHIRE TWO LADS...
Near CHESTERFIELD 1998
England's Yorks, Notts, Derbyshire workface is also its playground. A team scores a goal...

IN THE STREETS THE SCOTS
WERE DRESSED... SCOTLAND
V HOLLAND, ASTON VILLA,
ENGLAND EURO '96
... almost time for the football
after hours without.

ABOVE: ENGLAND 2 SCOTLAND 0
M6 MOTORWAY, ENGLAND EURO '96
Predictions of the game's outcome are widespread, since the countries haven't played each other in years.

LEFT: AND HE LIKED WHAT HE SAW
SCOTLAND V SWITZERLAND, AT ASTON VILLA, ENGLAND
EURO '96
The once feared and loathed tartan-kilted revellers again prove themselves to be masters at public relations.

MAIN PICTURE: GERMANY V RUSSIA
(ZEPPELIN PASSING OVERHEAD)
MANCHESTER UNITED, ENGLAND EURO '96
The foes of another war come feet to feet on hallowed turf, beneath the shadow of a mighty airship (beaming pictures to half of Europe).

RIGHT: **THE FATE OF THE RUSSIANS UNKNOWN**
V GERMANY, MANCHESTER UNITED, ENGLAND
EURO '96
Almost alone in a sea of Europeans all supporting other teams.

SCOTLAND V HOLLAND
ASTON VILLA, ENGLAND EURO '96
Half of Scotland and half of Holland find
the perfect occupation in a game of football in the English Midlands. The match
will end in a goal-less draw...

Later in this group stage, Holland will
be undone by England, yet squeeze
through on a single goal at the expense
of Scotland. Eventually the Dutch will be
put out by France in a penalty shoot-out
in Liverpool.

ENGLAND V SCOTLAND ... PENALTY SAVE
WEMBLEY STADIUM, ENGLAND EURO '96
England's Seaman dives the right way sending the ball spinning skyward - McAllister's experience is to no avail. His goalie can't bear to look.

A minute or so later and play will turn on him with a vengeance, tricked by blonde ambition in the form of Gazza.

ABOVE: BUILDING UP THEIR TEAM
ITALY V RUSSIA, LIVERPOOL, ENGLAND EURO '96
Fancily-dressed Italians compete with the official tannoy.

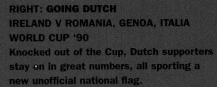

FOOTBALL TRUST BALLOON FEAST
ENGLAND V SWITZERLAND, WEMBLEY STADIUM, ENGLAND EURO '96
Football's biggest spenders (investors) The Football Trust celebrate the 'coming home' of the
game they have helped regenerate by giving grants to every League ground in the UK.
So far this decade £600 million has gone into redeveloping grounds and Wembley is the
showpiece arena. Dubbed 'The most famous ground in the world' Wembley will be rebuilt at
the turn of the century at a cost of £300 million, but at the expense of the twin towers.

RIGHT: **GOING DUTCH**
IRELAND V ROMANIA, GENOA, ITALIA
WORLD CUP '90
Knocked out of the Cup, Dutch supporters
stay on in great numbers, all sporting a
new unofficial national flag.

**ABOVE: ENGLAND AND COLOMBIA MAKE
A HEART OF IT**
LENS, FRANCE WORLD CUP '98
The ugly battleground outside suddenly gives way to
something beautiful within.

**LEFT: HUNGOVER FROM THE WAR
(THE NIGHT BEFORE)**
BOURNEMOUTH 1990
The domestic season comes to a head on the May
Bank Holiday, pairing relegation threatened
Bournemouth with Championship-chasing Leeds. The
town, awash with tourists, is terrorised by a police v
'fan' battle that has taken to the beaches for another
night. Some people (it was rumoured) had come here
to cause trouble - to use it as a 'landing exercise' for
Italia '90 only weeks away.

**RIGHT: A PAIR OF TICKETS FOR THE MATCH
BELGIUM V ENGLAND, BOLOGNA, ITALIA WORLD
CUP '90**
Everyone English is rounded up, strip-searched (if necessary), their cars emptied by the side of the road in a humiliating act for all to see and police guns are at the ready.

Meanwhile the locals saunter up to the Stadio Dall'Ara in the balmy evening air as if they're going to the opera - tickets tightly clutched.

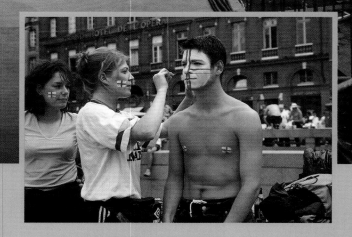

TOP: IMPRESSIONABLE ENGLISH FAN
V ROMANIA, TOULOUSE, FRANCE WORLD CUP '98
An English rose of the modern variety.

ABOVE: DUTCH BEACH GIRLS
V ARGENTINA, MARSEILLES, FRANCE WORLD CUP '98
To be a Holland supporter you had only to wear orange, go to
the beach, get sand in your clogs, dance for six hours to a
Dutch disco-football-karaoke... and then finally take in the
match itself. Beauty knows no pain?

TOP: ANTHEM
NIGERIA AT TUNIS, TUNISIA AFRICAN NATIONS CUP '94
Only the richest, most dedicated or self-exiled Nigerians have
made it here across the desert, and across seas, to pledge
support for their mother country at a time of political strife.

ABOVE: FACE-PAINTED NIPPLES
V ROMANIA, TOULOUSE, FRANCE WORLD CUP '98
England are just about to go into their second battle for pre-
eminence, having already faced-off with Tunisia at Marseilles.

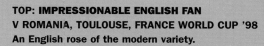

TOP: I GIVE YOU
NIGERIA AT TUNIS, TUNISIA AFRICAN NATIONS CUP '94
The 'Super Eagles' as they are known are making quite a name
for themselves on the football field. And these are members of
their official Supporters Club.

ABOVE: SLIGHT HESITATION
NIGERIA AT TUNIS, TUNISIA AFRICAN NATIONS CUP '94
The music stops for a moment due to a tumultuous display of
somersaults, collisions and cursed defending. Musicians whose
backs were turned, look over their shoulders.

TOP: MEXICAN IN ALL HIS GLORY
V BELGIUM, BORDEAUX, FRANCE WORLD CUP'98
Five hours to go until kick-off.

ABOVE: ENGLAND AND BEER
V ROMANIA, TOULOUSE, FRANCE WORLD CUP'98

MAIN PIC: FIESTA MEXICO AND HOLLAND
ST. ETIENNE, FRANCE WORLD CUP '98
It takes an open heart to enjoy such things in the aftermath of
the outcome of the match. A serious life-celebrating shindig
which some groups of supporters would never get to experience.

ABOVE: IRELAND V MEXICO (ON SACRED GROUND)
ORLANDO, USA WORLD CUP '94
In 110 degree heat the Irish players are knackered just walking to the centre-circle. Jack Charlton, their veteran manager, is later to fight it out with a FIFA match official over buckets of water for his boys in need.

The referee takes a moment to check that the Irish number eleven for kick-off, as the Mexicans thank God. It's almost an entirely Catholic affair.

LEFT: A PLAYER EMERGES FOR MEXICO... CALLED JESUS
V BELGIUM, BORDEAUX, FRANCE WORLD CUP '98
Played out on the cool Atlantic Coast, in one-hundred-degree-plus heat, aged Belgium take the lead against a monastic Mexico.

Waiting in the wings is the substitute Jesus who shall come on to change the match.

RIGHT: NO GOAL TURKEY GOING HOME
V PORTUGAL, NOTTINGHAM, ENGLAND
EURO '96
Despite all their promise, Turkey have not
scored a single goal on English soil. Now
they will be forgotten.

BELOW: MEXICAN MADONNA
V HOLLAND, ST. ETIENNE, FRANCE WORLD
CUP '98
A rush of blood in the last few minutes
saves Mexican blushes. The Dutch masters,
hardly break sweat for most of the game.
   The Mexicans sweep out onto the street
to confront their TV crews who are relaying
pictures live to the folks back home.
Breasts are bared.

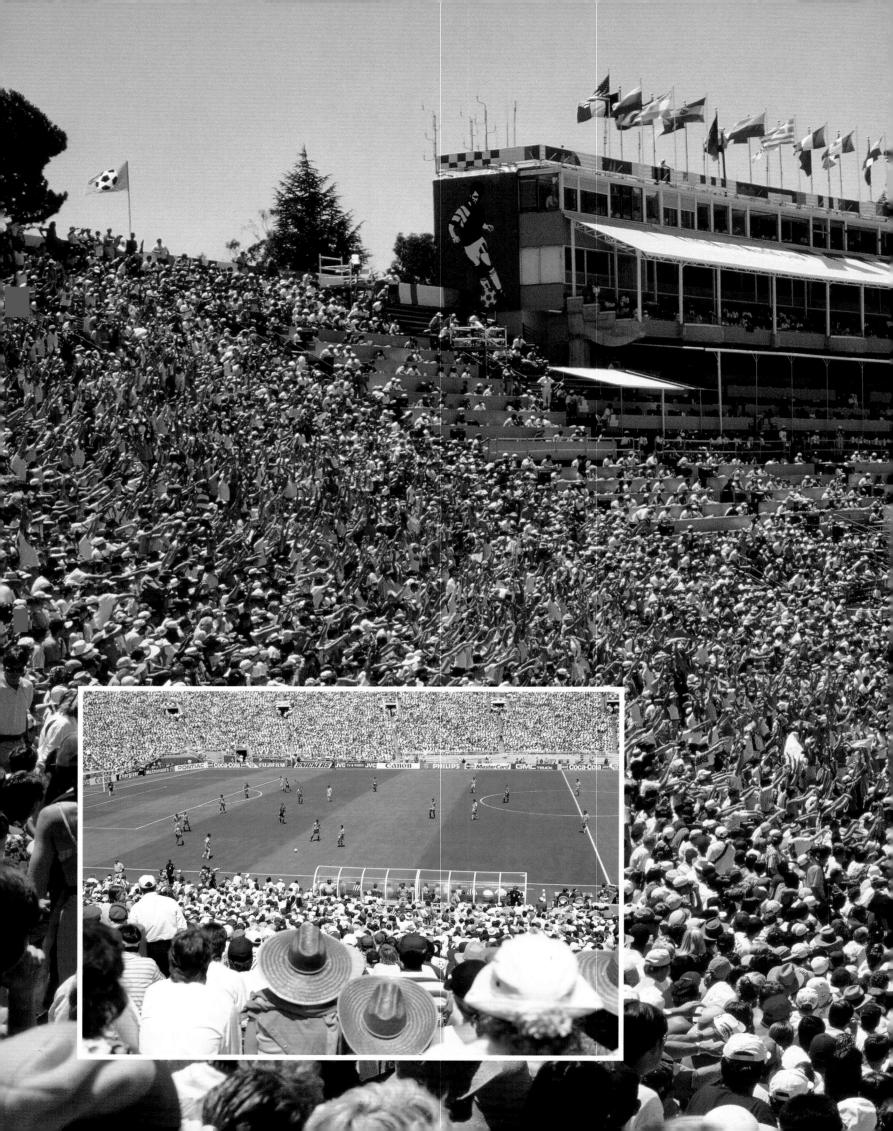

RUSSIAN AFRICAN MEXICAN WAVE
CAMEROON V RUSSIA, SAN FRANCISCO, USA WORLD CUP '94
The World Cup wave - which presumably began in Mexico all those years
ago - finally reaches this soccer-friendly coast.

TOP: J'Y ETAIS
FRANCE V CROATIA, ST. DENIS, FRANCE WORLD CUP '98
Croatia progress to the Semi-Finals in their first-ever World Cup,
and take their place in the league of nations, watched by
thousands in attendance and billions on TV worldwide.

For them it is not enough to merely say "I was there" but to
win and show their little nation off to all of the world.

ABOVE: ENGLAND TOURING TRIBES ARRIVE AT...
TOULOUSE, FRANCE WORLD CUP '98
Inside the City Hall a civic reception is interrupted by various
'Americans' who come to look at the balcony. In reality they are
daring English romeos who have come to exhibit messages of
love for their hometown to the thousands assembled in the
Square below.

Portsmouth, as with most acts of capture, are first to the fore.

INSET LEFT: ROMANIA AT A STROLL, IN THE ROSE BOWL
V U.S.A., LOS ANGELES, USA WORLD CUP '94
Having scored the opening goal in the heat bowl, against the
hosts in their centrepiece stadium and in front of a worldwide TV
audience, why not settle for 1-0?

The win would set Romania up as a footballing nation for a
decade to come.

33

ENGLAND CELEBRATE TUNISIA
MARSEILLES, FRANCE WORLD CUP '98
If it was all to end in tears (or tear-gas...) how better to remember England's campaign than against an azure sky.

ARGENTINA GET AWAY WITH IT
V JAPAN, TOULOUSE, FRANCE WORLD CUP '98
The South Americans, World Cup winners more than once, seem to flatter their Asian counterparts, giving them huge chunks of possession, before killing them off.

The Japanese fans, put on a stunning show of flag-support for their team as they greet them on their arrival to the World Cup stage. At the end of the game they stay behind to clear up any mess they may have made. After all, they'll be hosting the World Cup party in 2002.

LEFT: THE LOCALS GO ABOUT THEIR BUSINESS
FRANCE V BRAZIL, ST. DENIS, FRANCE
WORLD CUP '98
Late afternoon, Sunday 12th July, the day of the World Cup Final... France never thought France would reach the final. For some it means a delay to their bus journey.

RIGHT: LE FINALE SNOG ADIEU
FRANCE V BRAZIL, ST. DENIS, FRANCE
WORLD CUP '98
No hard feelings at the end of the day.

MAIN PICTURE: THE BOY FROM
GALASHIELS LEVELS THE SCORE
BRAZIL V SCOTLAND, ST.DENIS, FRANCE
WORLD CUP '98
...how a boy from smalltown Scotland
grew up to star before the biggest TV
audience ever.

FINGER ON THE TRIGGER

HANDSOME CAMERAMAN ON THE WALL

VIDEO TAKES THE LEAD

ENFIN TOUT TOUT TOUT EST PRET

BRAZILIANS IN OPEN TOP

YOUNG PARISIENNE DRAPED IN FLAG

VW OWNER BLOWS HIS OWN TRUMPET

LE ROADBLOCK

VW TOLD WHERE TO GO

THREE COLOURFUL YOUNG MEN MAKE BRAZIL CHAINS

TWO LADIES WITH ATTITUDE STRUT THEIR STUFF

HIDING BEHIND THE BUXOM REF

V-SIGN FOR PAPA

TWO YOUNG WOMEN IN PAINT EXCHANGE

TEENAGE GIRL GETS THE BALANCE OF THE PLAYER

DON'T CALL ME...

FUZZBALL AT THE FOOTBALL TILL

VIDEO-DUNCE

ONE MAN AND HIS TEAM

THREE GIRLS ENJOY THE EXPOSURE

THREE ROLLERSKATERS ALONE WITH THEIR SNAPS

THE CAN-CAN MEN

THE ERECT YOUNG LADIES

THE SWIRL OF UNDERGARMENTS

LES VOYEURS LIFTED BY THE SIGHT OF PLAYERS ARRIVING

FRENCH REBELLION IN THE MAKING

BRAZILIAN ORGY IN THE MAKING

BOY ON FATHER'S SHOULDERS

WOMAN KEEPS HER HAT ON

DAD AND SON ON THE BENCH SIP THE ATMOSPHERE

On the stadium scoreboard: BERTI VOGTS AND TERRY VENABLES ASK YOU TO RESPECT BOTH NATIONAL ANTHEMS. THANKYOU.

FOOTBALL'S SECOND COMING
ENGLAND V GERMANY, WEMBLEY STADIUM, ENGLAND
EURO '96
The cross of St. George, along with a song (inspired by The Homes of Football), cement a nation's image of itself when for so long being an England supporter was to support one particular town's team. Respect is observed for both national anthems, as Gazza pans the crowd, taking it all in. This might not come round again.

FRANCE WALK OUT
(V ITALY) ST.DENIS, FRANCE WORLD CUP'98
Would an early exit from the competition have led to rows of empty seats?
We will never know.

France, the hosts, having waltzed through their opening round of matches, now take on the slightly sleepy giants and three times World Cup winners Italy in the new national stadium. And they will win, progressing to the semi-finals...

LEFT: WITH A SPLASH OF FRENCHMAN
V NORWICH CITY, LEEDS UNITED 1992
Cantona helps United lift the last ever four
Division Football League title trophy. Elland
Road is returned to greatness.

His profound effect on English football
might inspire other managers and clubs to
go with the French...

LEFT: KING FOR A DAY
V LEICESTER CITY, NEWCASTLE UNITED
1993
The modest, diminutive and Chaplin-esque
Andy Cole has more than played his part in
delivering a trophy to St. James Park as
well as in the day's 7-1 victory over
Leicester.

And he will go on to break all transfer
records when he's sold to Manchester
United.

RIGHT: UNIFORM FOR A WORLD CUP CAMPAIGN
STOCKPORT COUNTY 1990

One of *the* great summers - everyone, it seems, is drawn to the Italian experience - football fervour is at its highest.

With weeks of term to go, the 'official' school uniform around Edgeley Park is white football shirts and the Three Lions crest of courage.

RIGHT: DIRE EXPECTATIONS?
CREWE ALEXANDRA 1990

Theirs is one of the worst League success stories of all. No cups of any significance have ever come to Gresty Road. To finish in the top half of Division Three would mean their best position this century.

But this fact belies a deeper truth, which is that the club kindles many of the players who go on to prove themselves with bigger clubs. They may only be dire for a while.

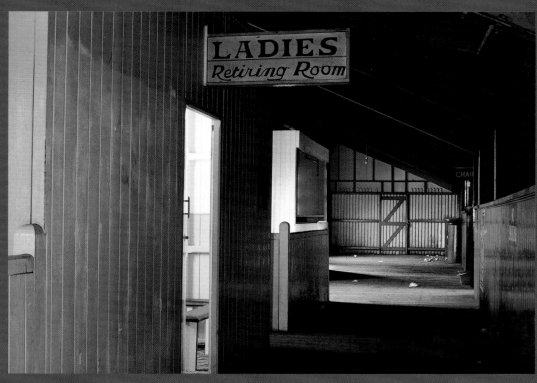

**LEFT: LADIES RETIRING ROOM
BURY 1990**
Gigg Lane carved out a niche for its womenfolk.

Years later the stand would be overhauled but, alas, with no similar facility.

RIGHT: SQUARE BALL
BOARDROOM
ROCHDALE 1990
A game man-managed throughout
the land.

THE MAN TO CHANGE EVERY GAME
V BARNSLEY, MANCHESTER UNITED 1997

TOP LEFT: CAMPING IT IN THEIR HALF
AUCHINLECK TALBOT V CUMNOCK 1994

MIDDLE LEFT: SPITTING, SWEARING AND CURSING CELEBRATION
AUCHINLECK TALBOT V CUMNOCK 1994
The fiercest of rivalries - two villages almost in each other's laps. Steel umbrellas are required as protection against the sorts of ammunition rained down upon each side.

   Old men chuckle at it all - they've survived countless campaigns.

BOTTOM LEFT: MEANWHILE BACK IN AYRSHIRE...
AUCHINLECK - CUMNOCK, SCOTLAND 1996

OPPOSITE TOP: CAMPED IN THEIR HALF
FORFAR ATHLETIC 1996

OPPOSITE BOTTOM: NEVER A MAN TO BE MOVED
FALKIRK V CELTIC, AT GLASGOW RANGERS 1997
Scottish Cup Semi-Final day and the man with a steeple on his shirt feels the Final chance falling to another kirk.

   But he of little faith will be proved pleasantly wrong.

ABOVE: A BEVVY OF KILLIE LASSES
KILMARNOCK V FALKIRK, AT GLASGOW RANGERS 1997
Girls from factories, Saturday shop assistants - whoever,
whatever - girls not normally to be seen at Killie
matches. But their presence adds a wonderful air of
innocence to the proceedings and reminds us why we
bother to revere our national cup competitions.

LEFT: DANCING IN THE STREETS OF ...
FALKIRK V KILMARNOCK, AT GLASGOW RANGERS 1997
Scottish Cup Final day for 'The Bairns' from a Scottish
smalltown.

LEFT: PETRIE IS LED AWAY
DUNFERMLINE ATHLETIC AT DUNDEE UNITED 1996
A wonderful end-of-term atmosphere pervades at
Tannadice, pushing players beyond their bounds. The
handsome Petrie is 'escorted from the pitch' - sent off
for his troubles.

BELOW: THE MENACE DISPERSED
DUNFERMLINE ATHLETIC AT DUNDEE UNITED 1996
Events outside the game ape the climax within.
Escorted from the match by his wife, Dunfermline's own
'Dennis the Menace' is saved from the comic antics of
various 'Desparate Dans' caked in Dundee
disappointment.

SCOTTISH CUP FINAL
HEART OF MIDLOTHIAN V RANGERS, HAMPDEN PARK 1996

GLASGOW'S FAVOURITE SONS STRUGGLE ON
(V AYR UNITED) PARTICK THISTLE 1998
One of the teams will go down on this, the last day of the season.

...fans just keep arriving, delaying kick-off, filling up both stands and forcing the police to open up one of the huge terraces not used for two years.

Partick not only face loss of status, but everything - all funds apparently spent on ground improvements.

TOP LEFT: THE GAME CHANGES SHAPE
MANCHESTER CITY 1993
They came to see a football match... and now this.

BOTTOM LEFT: A SHOW OF SCARVES (i)
V RANGERS, GLASGOW CELTIC 1997
Finally after years in the shadow of the Rangers-blue, Celtic
have the support, a stadium to match and a team to boot.

TOP RIGHT: DI CANIO BARES HIS SOUL
V RANGERS, GLASGOW CELTIC 1997
The crowd favourite D-I-S-C-O Di Canio the Italian, shows all
his flare, runs rings around everyone, then himself. Then
implodes.
   And on his way to an early bath (by way of the referee)
he will shove everyone in his path - even an adoring ball-boy
come to pat him.

BOTTOM RIGHT: POLICEMAN ASIDE THE OPEN KOP
V BLACKBURN ROVERS, SHEFFIELD WEDNESDAY 1993

ABOVE: WINTER'S LAST STAND
V ASTON VILLA, CRYSTAL PALACE 1990
It's a cold winter's day and the crowd - a big
one - survives the ten minutes of half-time by
nipping to the toilet, getting refreshments and
rocking-back and forth to keep warm. Palace,
(15th) are taking on Aston Villa - likewise
promoted and the current League leaders
ahead of Liverpool. The crowd (although it
might look big), is nothing compared to a day
in 1979 when in Division Two Burnley were
the opposition and the crowd totalled 51,482!

RIGHT: BURST THROUGH THE PALACE GATES
V WATFORD, CRYSTAL PALACE 1994
The fan is set to meet his maker.

LEFT: HIGH-KICKING CANTONA
MANCHESTER UNITED AT MANCHESTER
CITY 1996
United are storming all barricades...
and City slipping to relegation.

BELOW: LAST DAY ON THE HOLME
V WATFORD, CRYSTAL PALACE 1994
Safety measures will never again allow any
British ground to become really packed
(though some people undoubtedly enjoyed
standing, swaying and rubbing shoulders with
complete strangers).

Palace are Champions and promoted to
the Premiership for the coming season. The
huge uncovered Holmesdale Terrace
experiences its last ever stomp.

**MIDLAND'S SEMI-FINAL VENUE
CRYSTAL PALACE V LIVERPOOL
AT ASTON VILLA 1990**
The season heralds the return of
Aston Villa as a major force in
football. But it is as a semi-final
venue that many know the
ground and think of it as a sort
of Wembley of the Midlands.
Today 'David' has a re-match
with 'Goliath' having been
humiliated 9-0 earlier in the
season!
  The Palace balloons swirl
around the ground as Wright
and Bright lead the Palace
attack in one of the best
matches EVER.

RIGHT: CASTING ASPERSIONS IN THE TOILET AREA
EVERTON 1993
The Park Lane stand awaits another overhaul.

BELOW: HOME DRESSING ROOM
V CHELSEA, LIVERPOOL 1992
A worthy team is awaited ...

ABOVE: THE FLY PAST
BLACKBURN ROVERS OVER BURNLEY 1991
Although it's only half time in the semi-final play off
decider with Torquay United, some jokers from
neighbourhood rivals Blackburn reckon Burnley are to
remain sculling around the basement for at least another
season ... which turns out to be the case.

RIGHT: THE THINGS THAT CAN'T BE SAID
AT PLAINMOOR
TORQUAY UNITED V PLYMOUTH ARGYLE 1998

ABOVE: SENT TO COVENTRY BEAT, BY THE BULLENS
V COVENTRY CITY, EVERTON 1996
The mighty Everton struggle to beat 'these little teams'
these days. And their fans turn up in numbers to tell them
about it. *Nil Satis frustrated Evertonians.*

LEFT: ARSENAL CROWD RELIEVE THEMSELVES
V EVERTON, ARSENAL 1998
After winning two Championships at the turn of the
decade, it's a return to form for the Gunners.
   (Erstwhile Champions) Everton are but cannon fodder
on this day of Championship showmanship and
celebration in London.

RIGHT: DICKHEAD BURNS
V HIBERNIAN, CELTIC 1998
Ultimately failing to bag the big one (the Championship off Rangers) Tommy Burns is already on his way. There will always be detractors in football.

ABOVE: THE MANAGER QUESTIONS HIS CHAIRMAN
CARLISLE UNITED 1995
Mick Wadsworth has delivered his Chairman (and the City) a Championship winning-team
put together 'on a shoe-string' yet the Chairman has responded by pumping all the winnings
into redeveloping the stadium.

MAIN PICTURE: BUILDING ... THE STADIUM OF LIGHT
SUNDERLAND 1997
Lagging behind their near neighbours Boro and United, Sunderland suggest a move away
from Roker Park to an old mineface on the bend of the Wear and even nearer to town.
Mud, winds and rain hamper production.
   Then the sun comes out.

IF GOD LOOKED DOWN ON FOOTBALL
CARLISLE UNITED 1995
... he'd find United struggling to find the money for three more stands to justify the pitch being moved.

THE TEAM THAT MICK BUILT
CARLISLE UNITED 1995
'The Blues' are paraded in their innovative new
deck-chair strip, ahead of a Wembley appearance.
    The Cumbrian team of the decade.

**OF THE MANY GREAT STADIA
ON THE ROAD TO ROME, ITALIA WORLD CUP '90**
This is where the dream begins. It's a hell of a
long way down the hill to collect the ball!

INTERGALACTIC STADIUM COMES TO BOLTON
V EVERTON, BOLTON WANDERERS 1997
The first ever match at the new stadium will prove
to be goal-less. Although a Bolton shot does cross
the line. As shown on the multi-screen video-wall in
the corner of the ground.

LAST MATCH SEEN FROM THE CORNER
(V LUTON TOWN) MIDDLESBROUGH 1995
The opera singer Suzannah has sung her
aria (she's a life-long Boro fan to boot)...
The crowd has responded with *You'll
Never Walk Alone* and now it's time for
some football - the last they'll ever enjoy
(save in pictures) at Ayresome Park.
  The new Riverside Stadium beckons.

LEFT: PINK LADIES LINE-UP
CARLISLE LADIES 1996
A fledgling gaggle of girls get thrashed every
week in the name of football. So awful are they
in their new league, that to even get the ball
out of their half would be an achievement. And
to score a goal?!!! Two years on and the
newspaper reports, in its smallprint, news of a
victory - and then another, over North Eastern
opposition in League and Cup competition.

BELOW: PANORAMA OF FAST-DEVELOPING
DEEPDALE
V CHESTERFIELD, PRESTON NORTH END 1998
Deeply down some dale, without success for
decades and with a run-down series of Pavilions
and a piece of plastic passing for a pitch ... But
that was then and this is now - two new stands,
more on the way, a national football museum
and best of all, a team to make proud Preston
proud again.

RIGHT: ROY RACE SIGNS ON
V NOTTINGHAM FOREST, PORTSMOUTH 1992
FA Cup time again...

Legend has it that Christmas decorations only come down in Portsmouth public houses once the city's Pompey football team are out of the revered FA Cup (which could be well after Easter).

Their boys owned the FA Cup for longer than anyone, on account of those cancelled Cup years between 1940 to 1945. Someone had better do something about getting it back.

ABOVE: GOLIATH
NEWCASTLE UNITED AT SUNDERLAND 1992
The sort of unique colossus you'd pick for your team back then when you stood in
the school playground.

RIGHT: FINDING ONE'S LIKENESS IN THE CROWD
V NEWCASTLE UNITED, SUNDERLAND 1992

ELEVEN MENS' ACHIEVEMENT
FULHAM V WATFORD, CRAVEN COTTAGE 1998
The final day of the (Division Two) season pits Graham Taylor's Watford, already promoted, against Ray Wilkins' Fulham, who could yet go straight up. But if they don't, general manager Kevin Keegan is waiting in the wings.

ABOVE: NAIL-BITING EXPERIENCE
V STOKE CITY, PORT VALE 1998
Name your top-ten derby encounters in the land and
this one - even when so oft' a disappointment in terms
of footballing skill - must be on that list.

LEFT: FLICKING THE VICKEYS
PORT VALE AT STOKE CITY 1997
The last ever Potteries derby to be held at Stoke's
Victoria Ground, home of all City's history.
   Port Vale are, as ever, the supporting cast.

RIGHT: LAST GATHERING (VICTORIA GROUND)
V WEST BROMWICH ALBION, STOKE CITY 1997
The last few minutes before the old ship goes down -
it's soon to be bulldozed and redeveloped in the deal
to move up the road to The Brittannia Stadium where
a whole new hundred years of history will begin.

GREEN & PLEASANT LANDING
(V DENT) AMBLESIDE UNITED 1997
A thousand feet up atop Loughrigg, you can see everything and hear every shout and kick clearly - albeit an unearthly second later.

But if you lie on your back in the grass and try to follow the match by the tumult of sound alone you risk not seeing the G-OOOOO-AL in the actual second it was scored ... but it's a risk worth taking.

ABOVE: GOING AT IT AGAIN AND AGAIN
V LANGWATHBY, ULLSWATER UNITED 1998
In the valley, beside the Lake and against the backdrop of Place Fell, there is yet another team called United storming the leagues. And you can catch them playing almost every evening in April or May, as they try to catch up on the fixture backlog from a waterlogged winter.

LEFT: IN DEFENCE OF THE REALM
KESWICK 1997

**RIGHT: V LUNESDALE, AFORE SKIDDAW
BRAITHWAITE 1994**

**BELOW: AUGUST THIS LUSTFUL GAME
V CONISTON, AMBLESIDE UNITED 1998**
The cricket season has surrendered and winter's game
is once again in its rightful place and requisitioning
many of its versatile players who had been borrowed for
the summer.

   A huge crowd flocks to the Bank Holiday cup
encounter, in searing heat.

LEFT: **CRY FOR HOME**
GREENOCK MORTON V DUNFERMLINE ATHLETIC, 1995
The men of Cappielow have just defeated the League leaders in the sunshine.
    Then the rain and the cold blows in off the Clyde. Back to reality.

BELOW: **LET NO MAN MISTAKE HIS PLACE**
ROTHERHAM UNITED 1998
In Yorkshire they have a keen sense of what's where. And a keen tongue to boot.

ABOVE: DAYS BEFORE THE WINTER SHUT-DOWN
DERBY COUNTY 1992
Talk on the street is of moving away from The Baseball
Ground for ever ... while further afield, the talk is of
English football having an enforced winter break to
recharge its batteries - as well as other
'modernisations'.

LEFT: TURF MOOR CHIPPY
V TOTTENHAM HOTSPUR, BURNLEY 1993
Man looks down on his last customer.

LEFT: MOONLIGHT DRIVE HOME
V ARSENAL, COVENTRY CITY 1990
Thought unglamorous and seen as filling out Division One, Coventry actually became one of the top ten most successful sides on an aggregate of League achievements over the previous decade... a consistent record that holds them in good stead in the race for the much vaunted Super League. A league of few that could possibly see them favoured over such (former) giants as Everton.

Indeed, before the Millennium is out, Coventry unveil plans for one of the biggest, most expensive and fantastic new stadiums in the country with a capacity of well over 40,000.

BELOW: THE BURGER VENDOR
Traditional fayre on the way home.

LEFT: ENJOYING EACH OTHER'S COMPANY
LINFIELD V GLENTORAN, BELFAST 1994
The fiercest rivals (one team in bulletproof vests?) draw a big crowd on a warm spring day. Nothing could be better than football ...

RIGHT: DIGGING FOR GOLD UPON THE STONE
V PRESTON NORTH END, BRIGHTON & HOVE ALBION 1992
There are rewards to be had at 'ole Albion, if promotion can be secured ... and the shrinking of the ground put a stop to.

MAIN PICTURE: A MINUTE'S SILENCE FOR DIANA
V CARLISLE UNITED, BLACKPOOL 1997
The goalie has forgotten to join in the remembrance, so makes a dash for the centre-circle.

ABOVE: VIP GATHERING
V DERBY COUNTY, BLACKBURN ROVERS 1992
Someone on a tea-run from the Walker Steel Stand. A
few in the crowd will recall the great Jack Walker ...
in shorts ... and on the factory floor. Or driving past in
an old banger Cortina.

Ι They are left to revel in his spoils at £10 or so a
throw (the cost of a match-day ticket).

INSET MIDDLE RIGHT: BIG BOUNDARY GATHERING
V P.N.E., OLDHAM ATHLETIC 1998
Attendances at Boundary Park had slipped as the club
went into freefall down the Divisions.

Ι But neighbours Preston come and double the gate
and the scoreboard announcer hammers the FLASH
button in celebration.

**INSET BOTTOM RIGHT: SMALL BOUNDARY
GATHERING**
V P.N.E., OLDHAM ATHLETIC 1998
The couple's wedding reception, whether by accident
or design, coincides with the fans coming out of their
match.

**MAIN PIC: THE VALIANT ATHLETIC CHARLTON
CONGREGATION**
BRISTOL CITY 1994
Warm faces on a cold winter's day, fuelled by football
and banter.

Ι Without a Home ground to call their own (for so
many seasons), an Away trip can now be enjoyed
without the irony.

TOP LEFT: ENTRANCE FEE REVIEW
V ALBION ROVERS, ARBROATH 1996

MIDDLE LEFT: REPORTER WITH WIG
(V MOTHERWELL) HIBERNIAN 1995

BOTTOM LEFT: ERSTWHILE CLUB SHOP
ALLOA ATHLETIC 1996
Was it a voyage to the bottom of the sea and back for the club shop?

OPPOSITE TOP: COMING OF AGE PARTY
IN THE PADDOCK
V LEICESTER CITY, NEWCASTLE UNITED 1993

OPPOSITE BOTTOM: CRAWLING ABOUT ST. JAMES PARK
V MANSFIELD TOWN, EXETER CITY 1998
Having grovelled about 'under administration', the Grecians find a new lease of life in securing the future of their City centre ground and buying-up the adjacent school for future development.

ABOVE: **ROUTE ONE TACTICS**
WATFORD 1996
Watford had become known for their direct style of football under Graham Taylor.
And then he returned to oversee their re-birth.

OPPOSITE TOP LEFT: **THE GROUNDSMAN'S TOUCH**
LINCOLN CITY 1991
It's said that Sincil Bank, as with many grounds, has goal-mouths raised
an inch or three by the layer of human ashes sprinkled there.
   The groundsman goes about his business, adding flowers to an area
more accustomed to spit, swearing and kicking over the bucket during a
referee-induced tantrum.

OPPOSITE TOP RIGHT: **MY BROTHER KEVIN, BIG WATFORD FAN**
BACK GARDEN 1969
Kevin went on to create his own team, and build a full-size pitch in the
field behind our house (well before he'd ever seen or heard of Kevin
Costner in Field of Dreams).

OPPOSITE BOTTOM LEFT: **THE IRON-MAN IRONY ALL-YORKSHIRE
DERBY**
V LEEDS UNITED, SHEFFIELD UNITED 1990
The hard man of soccer, having only just transferred from Leeds to
Sheffield, gets both barrels from his new teammate (who will swop clubs
himself months later).

OPPOSITE BOTTOM RIGHT: **EMERGING FROM THE PUNCH-UP**
V LEEDS UNITED, SHEFFIELD UNITED 1990
No harm done; just a dust-up.

ABOVE: FOUR LADS OF SOUTH WALES
V LUTON TOWN, CARDIFF CITY 1994
The odd-one-out... Once upon a time they
won English FA Cup, once upon a time.

LEFT: NO RESPECT FOR UNITED
V LEEDS UNITED, MANCHESTER CITY
1993
Peter Reid sprints forward expecting his
Premier League charges to follow.

RIGHT: CORACLE TO FETCH THE BALL
V WATFORD, SHREWSBURY TOWN 1991

Shrewsbury's ground is right next to the River Severn. It is winter - cold and stormy. A man sits in his shadowy corner of the ground, close to a paddle. His job? Should the ball be hoofed into said river by some clumsy kicker, then our man J.E.D. (latest in a long line of Ds to do the job) must jump into the icy and fast-flowing river to retrieve the ball. Or balls. At £40 each the club cannot stand such losses.

On this day, however, there's no need for the boat or even the net with the long arm, as Shrewsbury are on target and plant every single shot into the Watford net, running-out 4-1 winners and bagging one of the big FA Cup upsets of the day.

BELOW: SWEAR IT'S FOOTBALL
V BLACKPOOL, NORTHAMPTON TOWN 1990

They too went up the Divisions... and down again. Visitors might be surprised to find the three-sided County ground sharing its patch with the cricket club. Surely out of sorts with the unique nature of football? And in the mid-nineties 'the Cobblers' moved their football out to Sixfields, down by the motorway and a custom-built stadium, not too dissimilar to an industrial unit.

And for the club - survival! And a chance to run up those divisions once more.

105

LEFT: CHEEKY MONKEY
V SUNDERLAND, BRISTOL CITY 1990

BELOW: UNITED COUNTER
V BARNSLEY, MANCHESTER UNITED 1997
... attack! Goes without saying, under Alex Ferguson.

Under his tutelage, Old Trafford has produced arguably the best, most entertaining teams in the history of (English) football.

**RIGHT: WE LIVE ON OAKWELL
BARNSLEY 1995**
A tradition of cats at Barnsley is continued when player Joe Joyce (hearing of the tradition but seeing no cats!) brings in a pair of sibling rivals.

LEFT: SIX-FOOTED TACKLE
CELTIC V RANGERS AT HAMPDEN PARK
1996
It takes three men to get the ball from
Gazza.

BELOW: GAZZA AND THE THREE GIRLS
RANGERS V HEARTS AT HAMPDEN PARK
1996
Rangers have stolen it 5-1 and autographs
are sought from the players emerging from
the dressing-rooms for interviews.

ABOVE: SHOW OF SCARVES (ii)
CELTIC V RANGERS 1997
Parkhead is on its way to filling out its
curves and ritually 'clothed' in green and
white for each match day occasion.

RIGHT: IN A MOUNTAIN SURROUND
CONISTON 1990
Shortly after this picture was taken a tree
was felled by a storm, taking the sign
with it and also bringing down the
infamous rickety-bridge (to be replaced
with a concrete one).

CONISTON
A·F·C

I N D E X

INDEX

THE TEAMWORK FINDS ITS SHINING STAR
V BARNSLEY, MANCHESTER UNITED 1997